United States Government Accountability Office

Report to Congressional Requesters

I0410944

September 2014

SECURE FLIGHT

TSA Could Take Additional Steps to Strengthen Privacy Oversight Mechanisms

GAO-14-647

September 2014

SECURE FLIGHT

TSA Could Take Additional Steps to Strengthen Privacy Oversight Mechanisms

Why GAO Did This Study

Since 2009, Secure Flight has changed from a program that identifies passengers as high risk solely by matching them against subsets of the TSDB, to one that uses PII and other information to assign passengers a risk category: high risk, low risk, or unknown risk. Secure Flight has established privacy oversight mechanisms to protect this PII.

GAO was asked to assess the current status of the Secure Flight program. In July 2014, GAO reported on the status of the program's operations, including changes to the program since 2009, implementation of Secure Flight screening determinations at airport checkpoints, and program performance measures. This report examines (1) the extent to which TSA has implemented privacy oversight mechanisms to address Secure Flight privacy requirements, and (2) the extent to which DHS's redress process addresses any delays and inconveniences that result from Secure Flight screening. GAO analyzed TSA data for fiscal years 2011 through 2013 and documents—including Secure Flight privacy training materials, documentation of privacy protections, and processing times for redress cases—and interviewed relevant DHS officials.

What GAO Recommends

GAO recommends that TSA provide job-specific privacy refresher training for Secure Flight staff and develop a mechanism to document and track key Secure Flight privacy issues and decisions. DHS concurred with GAO's recommendations.

View GAO-14-647. For more information, contact Jennifer A. Grover at (202) 512-7141 or GroverJ@gao.gov.

What GAO Found

The Transportation Security Administration (TSA) has taken steps to implement several of the privacy oversight mechanisms it planned to establish when Secure Flight implementation began in 2009, but additional actions could allow TSA to sustain and strengthen its efforts. Overall, TSA has implemented mechanisms to identify privacy implications associated with program operations and address them as necessary. For example, TSA has regularly updated privacy documents to address changes in the Secure Flight program. TSA has also implemented privacy training for new Secure Flight staff, and all Department of Homeland Security (DHS) employees receive annual privacy training. However, existing Secure Flight staff do not receive job-specific privacy refresher training consistent with Office of Management and Budget (OMB) requirements. Providing job-specific privacy refresher training could further strengthen Secure Flight's protection of personally identifiable information (PII). TSA also documents some aspects of its Secure Flight privacy oversight mechanisms, such as scheduled destructions of passenger data and reviews of planned changes to the Secure Flight system. However, TSA does not have a mechanism to comprehensively document and track key privacy-related issues and decisions that arise through the development and use of Secure Flight—a mechanism TSA planned to develop when Secure Flight was implemented in 2009. Comprehensively documenting and tracking key privacy-related issues and decisions, in accordance with federal internal control standards, could help TSA ensure that these decisions are carried into the future in the event of a change in personnel.

The DHS Traveler Redress Inquiry Program (DHS TRIP) affords passengers who may have been incorrectly matched to or listed on high-risk lists based on the Terrorist Screening Database (TSDB)—the U.S. government's consolidated list of known and suspected terrorists—an opportunity to seek redress. Passengers who, through the redress process, are determined to have been misidentified to a TSDB-based high-risk list are added to the TSA Cleared List, which allows them to be cleared (not identified as high risk) nearly 100 percent of time. The DHS TRIP process also allows passengers determined to have been improperly included on a TSDB-based list (mislisted) to be removed, minimizing the likelihood they will be identified as matches during future travels. Although DHS TRIP is not able to provide redress for passengers who may have been misidentified to high-risk, rules-based lists—TSA's lists of passengers who meet intelligence-driven criteria indicating they may pose a greater security risk—according to TSA officials, TSA procedures for using the lists mitigate impacts on these passengers. In fiscal year 2013, DHS TRIP began working to reduce processing time for its redress and appeals cases. In fiscal year 2014, DHS TRIP reduced its target for one of its key performance indicators—average number of days for DHS TRIP redress cases to be closed—from 93 to 78 days—and, for the first time, established a performance goal for the appeals process of 92 days. For fiscal years 2011 through 2013, the average total processing time for an appeals case was about 276 days. DHS TRIP plans to periodically review its progress in achieving its appeals performance goal and determine by February 2015 whether further changes to the appeals process are warranted.

Contents

Abbreviations

CBP	U.S. Customs and Border Protection
CDC	Centers for Disease Control and Prevention
DHS	Department of Homeland Security
FBI	Federal Bureau of Investigation
FIPPs	Fair Information Practices Principles
OIA	Office of Intelligence and Analysis
OMB	Office of Management and Budget
PIA	Privacy Impact Assessment
PII	personally identifiable information
RMS	Redress Management System
SFPD	Secure Flight Passenger Data
SORN	System of Records Notice
TRIP	Traveler Redress Inquiry Program
TSA	Transportation Security Administration
TSC	Terrorist Screening Center
TSDB	Terrorist Screening Database

GAO U.S. GOVERNMENT ACCOUNTABILITY OFFICE

441 G St. N.W.
Washington, DC 20548

September 9, 2014

The Honorable Michael T. McCaul
Chairman
The Honorable Bennie G. Thompson
Ranking Member
Committee on Homeland Security
House of Representatives

The Honorable Richard Hudson
Chairman
The Honorable Cedric L. Richmond
Ranking Member
Subcommittee on Transportation Security
Committee on Homeland Security
House of Representatives

The Honorable Mike Rogers
House of Representatives

The Transportation Security Administration's (TSA) Secure Flight program screens approximately 2 million passengers each day, matching passenger-provided personally identifiable information (PII) such as name and date of birth against federal government watchlists and other information to determine if passengers may pose a security risk and to assign them a risk category.[1] By identifying those passengers who may pose security risks, Secure Flight helps protect against potential acts of terrorism that might target the nation's civil aviation system. However, Secure Flight can also have inadvertent and potentially inappropriate impacts on the traveling public, such as when passengers are identified as high risk because they share a similar name and date of birth with an individual listed on a watchlist, and thus experience delays and inconveniences during their travels. In order to minimize such impacts on passengers, the Department of Homeland Security (DHS) Traveler Redress Inquiry Program (TRIP) provides an opportunity for travelers who

---

[1]PII is any information that permits the identity of an individual to be directly or indirectly inferred, including other information that is linked or linkable to an individual. See Department of Homeland Security, *Privacy Policy and Compliance*, DHS Instruction 047-01-001 (Washington, D.C.: July 25, 2011).

GAO-14-647 TSA Secure Flight Privacy

believe they have been delayed or inconvenienced because they have been incorrectly matched to or wrongly identified as the subject of certain watchlist records to seek redress. In addition, Secure Flight has privacy requirements that are intended to protect passengers' PII from unauthorized use or disclosure.

TSA developed and implemented Secure Flight in response to requirements in the Intelligence Reform and Terrorism Prevention Act of 2004, and a recommendation of the National Commission on Terrorist Attacks upon the United States (the 9/11 Commission) that TSA assume from air carriers the function of matching passengers against watchlists maintained by the federal government.[2] By assuming the matching functions previously performed by air carriers, Secure Flight was intended to, among other things, reduce the risk of unauthorized disclosure of sensitive watchlist information and better integrate information from DHS's existing traveler redress process into watchlist matching so that individuals would be less likely to be, for example, delayed or prohibited from boarding an aircraft. After initiating development of Secure Flight in August 2004, TSA began implementing it in 2009, and completed transitioning foreign and domestic air carriers to the program in November 2010.[3] Secure Flight now screens passengers and certain non-traveling individuals on all domestic and international commercial flights to, from, and within the United States; certain flights overflying the continental

---

[2]See Pub. L. No. 108-458, § 4012(a), 118 Stat. 3638, 3714-18 (2004) (codified at 49 U.S.C. § 44903(j)(2)(C)). The 9/11 Commission, *The 9/11 Commission Report: Final Report of the National Commission on Terrorist Attacks upon the United States*, July 2004. TSA efforts to develop a computer-assisted passenger prescreening system predated the Intelligence Reform and Terrorism Prevention Act and the report of the 9/11 Commission.

[3]TSA began implementing Secure Flight pursuant to the Secure Flight Program Final Rule, issued in October 2008. See 73 Fed. Reg. 64,018 (Oct. 28, 2008).

United States; and international point-to-point flights operated by U.S. aircraft operators.[4]

Beginning with a provision of the fiscal year 2004 Department of Homeland Security Appropriations Act and pursuant to requests by Congress, we have had regular and recurring responsibilities to assess and report on DHS's efforts to develop and implement a passenger prescreening program.[5] Our initial reports identified a number of challenges faced by TSA in developing this capability, including creating plans for managing and overseeing the Secure Flight program, coordinating with federal and private sector stakeholders, addressing key factors affecting system effectiveness, reducing program impacts on passenger privacy, and protecting passenger rights.[6] In May 2009, we found that after initial challenges, TSA had made significant strides in developing Secure Flight and that risks associated with implementing the program had been reduced.[7] For example, we found that TSA had made

---

[4]Secure Flight screens certain non-traveling individuals, such as escorts for minor, elderly, and disabled passengers, who are authorized to access the airport's sterile area—the portion of an airport defined in the airport security program that provides passengers access to boarding aircraft and to which access is generally controlled through the screening of persons and property. See 49 C.F.R. § 1540.5. Secure Flight began screening passengers on certain flights operated by foreign air carriers overflying the continental United States (excluding Alaska and Hawaii) on October 24, 2012. For purposes of this report, the term "commercial flight" encompasses all air carrier operations covered by and subject to the Secure Flight Final Rule. See 49 C.F.R. § 1560.3 (defining "covered flight" for purposes of the Secure Flight Program).

[5]GAO has performed this work in accordance with statutory mandates, beginning with the Department of Homeland Security Appropriations Act, 2004, Pub. L. No. 108-90, § 519, 117 Stat. 1137, 1155-56 (2003), and, most recently, the Department of Homeland Security Appropriations Act, 2009, Pub. L. No. 110-329, Div. D, § 512, 122 Stat. 3574, 3682-83 (2008), and pursuant to the requests of various congressional committees.

[6]GAO, *Aviation Security: Secure Flight Development and Testing Under Way, but Risks Should Be Managed as System Is Further Developed*, GAO-05-356 (Washington, D.C.: Mar. 28, 2005); *Aviation Security: Significant Management Challenges May Adversely Affect Implementation of the Transportation Security Administration's Secure Flight Program*, GAO-06-374T (Washington, D.C.: Feb. 9, 2006); *Aviation Security: Management Challenges Remain for the Transportation Security Administration's Secure Flight Program*, GAO-06-864T (Washington, D.C.: June 14, 2006); *Aviation Security: Transportation Security Administration Has Strengthened Planning to Guide Investments in Key Aviation Security Programs, but More Work Remains*, GAO-08-456T (Washington, D.C.: Feb. 28, 2008).

[7]GAO, *Aviation Security: TSA Has Completed Key Activities Associated with Implementing Secure Flight, but Additional Actions Are Needed to Mitigate Risks*, GAO-09-292 (Washington, D.C.: May 13, 2009).

progress with respect to establishing privacy protections to, among other things, ensure that PII maintained by the Secure Flight system (such as passenger name and date of birth) is properly collected, used, and stored. We also reported that TSA planned to use the redress process managed by DHS TRIP to assist passengers who may have been adversely affected by Secure Flight screening.[8]

In light of our prior work, you asked us to report upon the effectiveness of TSA's efforts to address Secure Flight system performance, privacy protections, and redress.

In July 2014, we issued a sensitive security information/law enforcement sensitive report on the performance of the Secure Flight program, including how the program has changed since implementation began in 2009, the extent to which Secure Flight vetting results are fully implemented at airport security checkpoints, and the extent to which TSA's performance measures appropriately assess progress toward achieving the Secure Flight program goals.[9]

This report addresses the following two questions:

1. To what extent has TSA implemented privacy oversight mechanisms to address Secure Flight privacy requirements?

2. To what extent is DHS's redress process addressing the delays and inconveniences that result from Secure Flight screening?

To answer our first question, we reviewed our 2009 report on Secure Flight's implementation, which identified the privacy oversight mechanisms that TSA planned to implement at that time.[10] We obtained

---

[8]DHS TRIP is a single point of contact for individuals who have inquiries or seek resolution regarding difficulties they experienced during their travel screening at transportation hubs—like airports and train stations—or crossing U.S. borders, including inspection problems at ports of entry and situations where travelers believe they have been unfairly or incorrectly delayed, denied boarding, or identified for additional screening or inspection at our nation's transportation hubs. While serving as the point of contact for the receipt, tracking, and response to redress applications, DHS TRIP refers cases to the appropriate agency for review and adjudication.

[9]We did not assess the extent to which Secure Flight vetting results for low-risk passengers are implemented at checkpoints.

[10]GAO-09-292.

and analyzed key TSA documents on these oversight mechanisms to assess TSA's progress in implementing them. Specifically, we reviewed the basic, advanced, and refresher privacy training materials that TSA uses to train Secure Flight staff and assessed these trainings against the Office of Management and Budget's (OMB) privacy training requirements and our assessment guide for reviewing training and development efforts in the federal government.[11] We also reviewed TSA's monthly purge status reports for the period from April 2012 through May 2013 to assess the extent to which TSA has purged Secure Flight passenger data in accordance with Secure Flight data retention requirements. In addition, to evaluate TSA's documentation of Secure Flight privacy issues and decisions, we reviewed relevant documents prepared by TSA privacy officials and contract staff, including privacy compliance validation reports for the period from April 2012 through April 2013, monthly status reports prepared by TSA's privacy contractor for the period from March 2013 through April 2014, and Secure Flight's Privacy Issue Tracker. We assessed these documents against *Standards for Internal Control in the Federal Government*.[12] To clarify our understanding of Secure Flight's privacy requirements and the mechanisms for monitoring compliance with these requirements, we reviewed key TSA documents that provide information on Secure Flight privacy requirements, such as management directives, the Secure Flight Privacy Rules of Behavior, and Secure Flight System of Records Notices and Privacy Impact Assessments, and interviewed Secure Flight privacy officials and a representative of the contract staff who are responsible for monitoring compliance with these requirements.

To answer our second question, we reviewed DHS TRIP standard operating procedures and other documentation related to the redress process, such as the standard letters DHS sends to redress applicants. To identify the outcomes of the DHS TRIP redress process, we reviewed

---

[11]GAO, *Human Capital: A Guide for Assessing Strategic Training and Development Efforts in the Federal Government*, GAO-04-546G (Washington, D.C.: March 2004). The guide summarizes elements of effective training programs and presents related questions on the components of the training and development process in four broad, interrelated components: (1) planning/front-end analysis, (2) design/development, (3) implementation, and (4) evaluation. These criteria remain useful today because they are the most recent relevant guidance available to assess how agencies plan, design, implement, and evaluate effective federal training and development programs.

[12]GAO, *Internal Control: Standards for Internal Control in the Federal Government*, GAO/AIMD-00-21.3.1 (Washington, D.C.: November 1999).

relevant DHS TRIP data for fiscal years 2011 through 2013 on the number of travelers who applied for redress and the number of redress cases DHS TRIP forwarded to the Terrorist Screening Center (TSC)—a multi-agency organization administered by the Federal Bureau of Investigation (FBI)—for review. We also reviewed TSC data on the extent to which redress applications resulted in individuals being delisted from certain watchlists, meaning that they were removed from a watchlist because TSC determined that they did not meet current criteria for inclusion on that watchlist. To determine the extent to which DHS TRIP is meeting performance goals for the redress process, we reviewed DHS TRIP performance data. Additionally, to determine the extent to which DHS TRIP is meeting its performance goal for processing appeals cases, we calculated the average processing time for 49 closed appeals cases DHS TRIP received during fiscal years 2011 through 2013, using DHS TRIP data, and compared this average with the goal. To assess the reliability of DHS TRIP redress and appeals data, we examined documentation about these data, interviewed knowledgeable officials, and reviewed the data for obvious errors and inconsistencies. To further assess the reliability of the appeals data used to calculate average processing times, we compared the DHS TRIP data with data on appeals cases maintained by TSC, which reviews and makes recommendations on appeals, and followed up on any discrepancies. Although there were some discrepancies, we determined that the data were sufficiently reliable for the purpose of comparison to the performance goal. To better understand redress and appeals procedures and DHS TRIP's efforts to reduce processing time, we interviewed DHS TRIP and TSC officials. To better understand TSA's attempts to assist individuals for whom the DHS TRIP process cannot provide redress (i.e., individuals misidentified to the rules-based high-risk lists discussed later in this report), we interviewed DHS TRIP and TSA Office of Intelligence and Analysis officials.

We conducted this performance audit from March to September 2014 in accordance with generally accepted government auditing standards. Those standards require that we plan and perform the audit to obtain sufficient, appropriate evidence to provide a reasonable basis for our findings and conclusions based on our audit objectives. We believe that the evidence obtained provides a reasonable basis for our findings and conclusions based on our audit objectives.

Background

The Secure Flight program, as implemented pursuant to the 2008 Secure Flight Final Rule, requires commercial aircraft operators traveling to, from, within, or overflying the United States to collect information from passengers and transmit that information electronically to TSA.[13] This information, known collectively as Secure Flight Passenger Data (SFPD), includes PII, including full name, gender, date of birth, passport information, and certain non-personally identifiable information provided by the airline, such as itinerary information and the unique number associated with a travel record (record number locator).[14]

The Secure Flight program uses SFPD to screen passengers and assign them a risk category: high risk, low risk, or unknown risk. Table 1 describes Secure Flight's primary screening activities.

Table 1: Secure Flight Screening Activities

Screening Activity	Description
No Fly List (high risk)	The No Fly List is a subset of the Terrorist Screening Database (TSDB), the U.S. government's consolidated watchlist of known or suspected terrorists maintained by the Terrorist Screening Center (TSC), a multi-agency organization administered by the Federal Bureau of Investigation. The No Fly List contains records of individuals who are suspected or known to pose a threat to aviation or national security and are prohibited from boarding an aircraft or entering the sterile area of an airport.[a] Secure Flight has matched passengers against the No Fly List since 2009.
Selectee List (high risk)	The Selectee List is a subset of the TSDB containing records of individuals who must undergo additional security screening before being permitted to enter the sterile area or board an aircraft. Secure Flight has matched against the Selectee List since 2009.
Expanded Selectee List (high risk)	The Expanded Selectee List includes terrorist records in the TSDB with a complete name and date of birth that meet the reasonable suspicion standard to be considered a known or suspected terrorist, but that do not meet the criteria to be placed on the No Fly or Selectee Lists. Secure Flight began matching against the Expanded Selectee List in April 2011.[b]
Transportation Security Administration (TSA) rules-based lists (high risk)	The high-risk rules-based lists include two lists of passengers who may not be known or suspected terrorists, but who, according to intelligence-driven, scenario-based rules developed by TSA in consultation with U.S. Customs and Border Protection (CBP), may pose an increased risk to transportation or national security.

[13]For purposes of this report, the term "commercial aircraft operator" includes the passenger operations of a U.S.- and foreign-flagged air carrier operating in accordance with 49 C.F.R. §§ 1544.101(a) and 1546.101(a)-(b), respectively (also referred to as a "covered aircraft operator"). See 49 C.F.R. § 1560.3.

[14]See 49 C.F.R. § 1560.3. Aircraft operators must transmit available SFPD to Secure Flight approximately 72 hours prior to scheduled flight departure. For reservations created within 72 hours of flight departure, aircraft operators must submit passenger data as soon as they become available.

Screening Activity	Description
Centers for Disease Control and Prevention (CDC) Do Not Board List (high risk)	The CDC Do Not Board List is managed by CDC. It includes individuals who pose a significant health risk to other travelers and are not allowed to fly.
TSA Pre✓™ lists (low risk)	TSA Pre✓™ lists include lists of pre-approved, low-risk travelers, such as certain members of CBP's Trusted Traveler programs, members of the U.S. armed forces, Congressional Medal of Honor Society members, and Members of Congress—groups of individuals TSA has determined pose a low risk to transportation or national security—as well as a TSA Pre✓™ list, created by TSA and composed of individuals who apply and are pre-approved as low-risk travelers through the TSA Pre✓™ Application Program.[c] Secure Flight began matching against its first set of low-risk lists, CBP Trusted Traveler Lists, in October 2011 and instituted the TSA Pre✓™ Application Program in December 2013.
TSA Pre✓™ Disqualification List (ineligible for low risk)	The TSA Pre✓™ Disqualification List is a list of individuals who, based upon their involvement in violations of security regulations of sufficient severity or frequency, are disqualified from receiving expedited screening for some period of time or permanently (e.g., bringing a loaded firearm to the checkpoint).
TSA Pre✓™ risk assessments (low risk)	Secure Flight assesses certain travel-related information submitted by passengers and assigns them scores that correspond to a likelihood of being eligible for expedited screening for a specific flight. Secure Flight began performing these assessments for select frequent flier members in October 2011 and, in October 2013, began using them to evaluate all passengers not determined to be a match to a high-risk or low-risk list.

Source: GAO analysis of TSA and TSC information. | GAO-14-647

[a]In general, the "sterile area" is the portion of an airport beyond the security screening checkpoint that provides passengers access to boarding aircraft and to which access is generally controlled through the screening of persons or property. See 49 C.F.R. § 1540.5.

[b]All TSDB-based watchlists utilized by the Secure Flight program contain records determined to have met TSC's reasonable suspicion standard. In general, to meet the reasonable suspicion standard, the agency nominating an individual for inclusion in the TSDB must consider the totality of information available that, taken together with rational inferences from that information, reasonably warrants a determination that an individual is known or suspected to be or have been knowingly engaged in conduct constituting, in preparation for, in aid of, or related to terrorism or terrorist activities. As previously discussed, to be included on the No Fly and Selectee Lists, individuals must meet criteria specific to these lists. The TSDB, which is the U.S. government's consolidated watchlist of known or suspected terrorists, also contains records on additional populations of individuals that do not meet the reasonable suspicion standard articulated above, but that other federal agencies utilize to support their border and immigration screening missions. In addition, according to TSA officials, Secure Flight does not utilize all terrorist records in the TSDB because records with partial data (i.e., without first name, surname, and date of birth) could result in a significant increase in the number of passengers misidentified as being on the watchlist and potentially cause unwarranted delay or inconvenience to travelers.

[c]Individuals on all low-risk lists receive a Known Traveler Number that they must submit when making travel reservations to be identified as low-risk. See 49 C.F.R. § 1560.3 (defining "Known Traveler Number"). TSA also refers to these lists as Known Traveler lists.

Secure Flight screening against watchlists involves the automated comparison of SFPD and list data and a manual review process by Secure Flight analysts of all passengers identified by the system as potential matches. Air carriers may not issue a boarding pass to a passenger who is a potential match to the No Fly or Selectee lists until they receive from Secure Flight a final determination on how the passenger will be screened at the checkpoint if provided a boarding pass.

These determinations include a "TSA Pre✓™ eligible" message for passengers who may receive expedited screening; a "cleared" message for passengers found not to match any high or low-risk list and who, therefore, will receive standard screening; and a "selectee" message for passengers who are to be selected for additional screening.[15] For passengers matching the No Fly List, the air carrier may not issue a boarding pass.

Secure Flight Privacy Requirements

Statutory requirements govern the protection of PII by federal agencies, including the use of air passengers' information by Secure Flight. For example, the Privacy Act of 1974 places limitations on agencies' collection, disclosure, and use of personal information maintained in systems of records.[16] Among other things, the Privacy Act requires agencies to publish a notice—known as a System of Records Notice (SORN)—in the Federal Register describing such things as the type of personal information collected, the types of individuals about whom information is collected, the intended "routine" use of the data, and procedures that individuals can use to review and correct personal information. Also, the E-Government Act of 2002 requires agencies to conduct Privacy Impact Assessments (PIA) that analyze how personal information is collected, stored, shared, and managed in a federal system.[17] Agencies are required to make their PIAs publicly available if practicable. In May 2009, we reported that TSA had published required privacy documents, such as the PIA and SORN, that discuss the purposes, uses, and protections for passenger data, and outline which

---

[15]Standard screening typically includes passing through a walk-through metal detector or Advanced Imaging Technology screening, which identifies objects or anomalies on the outside of the body, and X-ray screening for the passenger's accessible property. Enhanced screening includes, in addition to the procedures applied during a typical standard screening experience, a pat-down and an explosive trace detection search or physical search of the interior of the passenger's accessible property, electronics, and footwear. Expedited screening typically includes walk-through metal detector screening and X-ray screening of the passenger's accessible property, but unlike in standard screening, travelers do not have to, among other things, remove their belts, shoes, or light outerwear. The Secure Flight system may also return an error response to air carriers regarding passengers for whom Secure Flight has received incomplete data.

[16]A system of records is any item or grouping of information about an individual under the control of an agency from which information is retrieved by the name of the individual or some number or other identifying particular. See 5 U.S.C. § 552a(a)(5).

[17]See Pub. L. No. 107-347, § 208, 116 Stat. 2899, 2921-23 (2002).

data elements are to be collected and from whom.[18] TSA has since published three updates to the Secure Flight PIA and two updates to the Secure Flight SORN.

DHS privacy policies also govern Secure Flight's handling of passenger information. For example, since 2008, it has been DHS policy to follow the Fair Information Practices Principles (FIPPs), which provide a framework for balancing the need for privacy with other public policy interests, such as national security and law enforcement.[19] (See app. I for a description of the FIPPs.)

Redress for Secure Flight

DHS established DHS TRIP in February 2007 as the central processing point within DHS for travel-related redress inquiries.[20] DHS TRIP provides passengers who believe they have been unfairly or incorrectly delayed, denied boarding, or identified for additional screening with an opportunity to be cleared if they are determined not to be a match to TSDB-based watchlist records (i.e., misidentified) or if they have been wrongly identified as the subject of a TSDB watchlist record (i.e., mislisted). Passengers apply to DHS TRIP using an online application, by e-mail, or by mail. Upon receipt of a complete application, DHS TRIP sends a notification of receipt with a redress control number to the passenger. DHS TRIP adds the name, date of birth, and redress control number of applicants determined not to match a TSDB-based list to the TSA Cleared List. Passengers included on the TSA Cleared List must then submit their redress control number when making a reservation to allow the Secure Flight system to recognize and clear them. However, if DHS TRIP determines that an individual is still a potential match to a TSDB watchlist

---

[18]GAO-09-292.

[19]See DHS, *The Fair Information Practice Principles: Framework for Privacy Policy at the Department of Homeland Security,* DHS Privacy Policy Guidance Memorandum 2008-01 (Washington, D.C., Dec. 29, 2008), and DHS, *Privacy Policy and Compliance,* DHS Directive 047-01-001 (Washington, D.C., July 25, 2011). The FIPPs, a set of principles first proposed in 1973 by a U.S. government advisory committee, are used with some variation by organizations to address privacy considerations in their business practices and are also the basis of privacy laws and related policies in many countries, including the United States, Australia, and New Zealand, and in the European Union.

[20]Pursuant to the Intelligence Reform and Terrorism Prevention Act, TSA was to establish a timely and fair process for individuals identified as a threat as a result of TSA's passenger prescreening system to appeal to TSA the determination and correct any erroneous information. See 49 U.S.C. § 44903(j)(2)(G)(i).

GAO-14-647 TSA Secure Flight Privacy

record, it refers the matter to TSC for further review. TSC then conducts its own review of whether the individual has been misidentified to a watchlist and should be added to the TSA Cleared List. If TSC determines that the individual was correctly matched to a watchlist, TSC then reviews, based on the most current available information and criteria for inclusion on the list, whether the individual is either correctly assigned to the list, or is wrongly assigned and should be removed from the list. If DHS TRIP and TSC determine that no change in the passenger's status is warranted, the passenger is notified of this decision, and depending on the determination, some passengers are permitted the opportunity to appeal the decision.[21] Applicants eligible for appeals receive a letter providing instruction on how to engage in the process, which is carried out by DHS TRIP and TSC.

TSA Has Implemented Oversight Mechanisms to Address Passenger Privacy Requirements, but Additional Actions Could Better Ensure Full Compliance

TSA has taken steps to implement several of the privacy oversight mechanisms it planned to establish in 2009, when Secure Flight implementation began, but additional actions could allow TSA to sustain and strengthen its efforts. In May 2009, we found that TSA had taken actions that generally addressed the FIPPs, such as instituting access controls to ensure that data are not accidentally or maliciously altered or destroyed, filtering unauthorized data from incoming data to ensure collection is limited to predefined types of information, and developing incident response procedures to address and contain privacy incidents. We also reported that TSA had designated a program privacy officer and a team of privacy experts to work on various aspects of the Secure Flight program, and planned to establish several privacy oversight mechanisms, including the following:

- privacy rules of behavior, which require that individuals handling PII use it only for a stated purpose;[22]
- audit logs of system and user events to provide oversight of system activities, such as access to PII and transfer of PII into or out of the system;

---

[21]The types of passengers who are permitted to appeal this decision are considered sensitive security information.

[22]SFPD includes several data elements that are considered PII—passenger name, date of birth, gender, and passport information; it also includes non-PII data, such as itinerary information and the unique number associated with a travel record (record locator number). See 49 C.F.R. § 1560.3.

- general privacy training for all Secure Flight staff and role-based privacy training for employees handling PII;
- periodic privacy compliance reports, intended to track and aggregate privacy concerns or incidents; and
- a system for tracking privacy issues that arise throughout the development and use of Secure Flight, and conducting follow-up analysis of significant privacy issues and providing resolution strategies for management consideration.

Since our May 2009 report, TSA has made progress in implementing some of these privacy oversight mechanisms, although more work remains to fully implement them. Overall, the Secure Flight privacy team, composed of TSA's Privacy Officer, the designated Secure Flight program privacy officer, TSA's Office of the Chief Counsel, and dedicated contract staff, has worked closely with the DHS Privacy Office to ensure periodic consultation on program plans and operations that may have privacy implications.[23] The publication of revised PIAs and SORNs to address the changes in the Secure Flight program, such as the use of rules-based high-risk lists and TSA Pre✓ ™ risk assessments, is evidence of this consultation process. TSA issued Secure Flight Privacy Rules of Behavior in September 2008 that set forth the practices staff (including federal employees, contractors, and other persons authorized to access or use SFPD) should follow in accessing, using, maintaining or collecting Secure Flight PII. According to TSA officials, in 2013, TSA initiated a review of the rules of behavior to ensure that they still align with current Secure Flight directives and practices, which have changed since the rules of behavior were first issued in 2008. In May 2014, TSA officials stated that they are in the final stages of developing an updated version of the Privacy Rules of Behavior. In December 2013, TSA also issued a management directive discussing TSA's policy for responding to requests for Secure Flight data by TSA employees and other agencies. Secure Flight also maintains audit logs of Secure Flight system and user events, as it planned to do in 2009. Specifically, TSA maintains logs of

- successful and unsuccessful log in attempts to access the component of Secure Flight that allows carriers to submit passenger information via the Internet, known as eSecure Flight;

---

[23]According to TSA officials, the Secure Flight program privacy officer also currently serves as the Secure Flight program manager, and is therefore well-informed about Secure Flight operations and well-positioned to implement privacy decisions.

- the Secure Flight User Interface, which is the system Secure Flight analysts use to retrieve passenger data and review potential matches; and
- requests to access the Report Management System, which generates reports on Secure Flight activities.

According to Secure Flight privacy officials, the TSA Security Operations Center monitors these logs 24 hours a day, 7 days a week. Officials stated that these logs allow TSA to be aware of any attempts to gain unauthorized access to the system and can be used to make adjustments in access controls, should they be needed, in response to identified threats.

TSA has also implemented privacy training for new Secure Flight staff and documented privacy issues and decisions through, for example, periodic compliance privacy reports. However, additional actions could allow TSA to sustain and strengthen its efforts to ensure compliance with Secure Flight privacy requirements.

Privacy training for Secure Flight staff: TSA has developed and implemented basic and advanced privacy training that, according to TSA officials, is required for all new Secure Flight staff.[24] In addition, all DHS staff are required to complete annual DHS privacy training, which discusses the importance of safeguarding PII. However, Secure Flight staff do not receive job-specific privacy refresher training after they complete the initial Secure Flight training. OMB requires agencies to train employees on their privacy and security responsibilities before permitting access to agency information and information systems, and thereafter to provide at least annual refresher training to ensure employees continue to understand their responsibilities.[25] The OMB memorandum also states that this refresher training must be job-specific and commensurate with the employee's responsibilities. TSA officials stated that the annual DHS

---

[24]The basic training course covers practices for the collection, use, and safeguarding of PII. The advanced training addresses the additional privacy responsibilities required of Secure Flight Operations Center analysts—who work independently and with air carriers to resolve system matching results and thus deal extensively with passenger PII—and information technology staff for the use, sharing, protection, retention, and destruction of PII.

[25]Office of Management and Budget, *Safeguarding Against and Responding to the Breach of Personally Identifiable Information,* OMB Memorandum M-07-16 (Washington, D.C.: 2007).

privacy training serves as refresher training for Secure Flight staff. However, DHS's annual refresher training is not job-specific and does not reflect the unique privacy requirements of the Secure Flight program. For example, the DHS training provides a general overview of privacy requirements Department-wide, but does not provide information on the unique privacy risks of the Secure Flight program, such as the potential misuse or unauthorized disclosure of airline passenger data. Furthermore, the Secure Flight program has expanded from a program that solely identifies high-risk passengers on the No Fly and Selectee Lists to one that also identifies additional high-risk passengers using other records in the TSDB and through rules-based high-risk lists, as well as low-risk passengers. TSA's PIAs for these new screening activities discuss new privacy risks unique to these activities. For example, Secure Flight's September 2013 PIA update discusses the importance of restricting the use and dissemination of TSA Pre✓™ lists in order to mitigate the risk associated with collecting and storing information on low-risk travelers. TSA officials told us that TSA updated its privacy training for new Secure Flight staff in December 2013 to reflect Secure Flight's updated PIAs and SORNs. However, because the DHS privacy refresher training is not job-specific, staff who joined Secure Flight prior to December 2013, when TSA updated its privacy training for new staff, may not have received privacy training specific to Secure Flight's new screening activities. Our assessment guide for reviewing training and development efforts in the federal government states that changes, such as new initiatives, technological innovations, or reorganizations and restructuring, will likely require agencies to develop new or revised training programs, and that agencies should have a formal process for incorporating these strategic and tactical changes to ensure that new and revised training efforts are quickly brought on line.[26] Providing at least annual job-specific privacy refresher training, consistent with OMB requirements, could further strengthen Secure Flight's protection of PII.

Documenting privacy issues: TSA documents some aspects of its privacy oversight mechanisms, such as scheduled destructions of SFPD and reviews of planned changes to the Secure Flight system. However, TSA does not have a mechanism to comprehensively document and track key privacy-related issues and decisions that arise through the

---

[26]GAO-04-546G.

development and use of Secure Flight—a mechanism TSA planned to develop when Secure Flight was implemented in 2009.

First, TSA prepares purge reports to document the monthly destruction of SFPD in accordance with Secure Flight's data retention schedule. We requested and reviewed documentation for the 14-month period from April 2012 through May 2013. The documentation showed that TSA consistently purged passenger records in accordance with its retention schedule, with the exception of a 2-month period.[27]

Second, Secure Flight privacy staff members prepare privacy compliance validation reports to document privacy concerns or issues that are raised by staff in the software development process. According to Secure Flight officials, a proposed change to the Secure Flight system cannot be implemented until the privacy team completes a compliance validation report, which includes a summary of privacy findings, conclusions, and recommendations for corrective measures. For example, two of the eight reports we reviewed for the period from April 2012 through April 2013 identified a potential privacy issue in Secure Flight's plans to conduct TSA Pre✓™ risk assessments. Specifically, the March and April 2013 reports stated that Secure Flight should not begin conducting these assessments until the new PIA and SORN were approved.[28]

Last, Secure Flight privacy staff also maintain a set of notes regarding some privacy issues or privacy-related tasks. These notes, referred to collectively as the Privacy Issue Tracker, do not describe the nature, basis, or resolution of the issues, nor do they aggregate all privacy concerns raised by staff or the key decisions made in response, such as concerns about TSA's plans to conduct TSA Pre✓™ risk assessments, discussed in the March and April 2013 compliance validation reports. Secure Flight privacy officials stated that TSA did not intend for the Privacy Issue Tracker to serve as the agency's system for systematically tracking Secure Flight privacy issues and incidents.

---

[27]There was a 2-month period in 2012 when the automated purge reports were inoperable because the generation of these reports was slowing overall Secure Flight system performance and causing instability in the Secure Flight system. During this period, TSA was unable to validate that purges of passenger PII were occurring in accordance with the agreed-upon schedules. Once a fix was implemented, TSA was able to review the purge reports retroactively and confirm that there were no purge violations.

[28]Both reports concluded that upon approval and publication of the updated privacy impact assessment and system of records notice, there would be no privacy concerns with the release of the new software.

In the absence of a system for comprehensively documenting and tracking privacy-related issues and decisions, TSA's Secure Flight privacy officer stated that Secure Flight relies on its privacy contract staff to oversee and monitor privacy protections, in consultation with the designated Secure Flight program privacy officer and the TSA Privacy Officer. The privacy contract staff are broadly tasked with ensuring compliance with Secure Flight's privacy policies and requirements, identifying privacy issues, and providing resolution strategies for management consideration. According to TSA officials, the contract staff accomplish this through being embedded in the day-to-day operations of the Secure Flight program. For example, the contract staff attend meetings in which Secure Flight software or system changes are being discussed to ensure that the planned software update remains within the scope of the Secure Flight program mission and that prior to deployment, a software release has no privacy concerns or that any concerns have been resolved or mitigated. Contract staff also issue monthly status reports, which provide an overview of contractors' accomplishments and planned activities. These reports refer to ongoing privacy issues, but according to TSA officials, were not intended to consistently describe the nature, basis, or resolution of these issues. According to TSA's Privacy Officer and the contract staff we spoke with, the contract staff recognize the potential for privacy issues based on their experience and professional judgment, and raise the issues as appropriate. Officials also stated that most privacy issues are resolved through discussions. Additionally, the TSA Privacy Officer stated that the frequent interaction between the contract staff, program privacy officer, and TSA Privacy Officer creates a robust understanding of Secure Flight operations and plans. However, it is unknown whether this ad hoc communication between key Secure Flight privacy staff would be sustained after a personnel change in Secure Flight's privacy team or contractor personnel, and whether privacy-related decisions previously made would continue to be implemented without documentation to inform new staff. Further, TSA previously stated that it would institute a system for tracking privacy issues that arise throughout the development and use of Secure Flight. By institutionalizing such a mechanism, TSA would have greater assurance that its oversight of Secure Flight privacy protections is effective because TSA would know the extent to which privacy issues are identified and resolved.

DHS has established a department-wide Online Incident Handling System to document and track information on DHS privacy incidents, which would include incidents related to the Secure Flight program.[29] TSA and Secure Flight privacy officials stated that there have not been any privacy incidents, such as unauthorized disclosures, uses, or modifications of PII, since Secure Flight implementation began in January 2009.[30] However, should the Secure Flight program become aware of a privacy incident, the TSA Privacy Officer would be required to submit a Privacy Incident Report in the Online Incident Handling System, thereby notifying senior DHS officials of the incident. Though these Privacy Incident Reports would track suspected and confirmed incidents involving PII (e.g., unauthorized disclosure or access of PII), according to DHS officials, they were not intended to address privacy issues that arise in the development and use of Secure Flight when they do not rise to the level of an incident, such as the potential privacy issues Secure Flight identified when reviewing system changes. Therefore, the DHS Online Incident Handling System does not document efforts by Secure Flight officials to identify and address issues before they result in an incident.

Standards for Internal Control in the Federal Government calls for federal agencies to design and implement control activities to enforce management's directives and to monitor the effectiveness of those controls.[31] Recording and documenting key decisions are among the suite of control activities that are an essential part of an agency's planning, implementing, and reviewing, and they are essential for proper stewardship and accountability for government resources and achieving efficient and effective program results. Comprehensively documenting and tracking key privacy issues and decisions, as TSA planned when Secure Flight implementation began in 2009, could help ensure that these decisions, which have allowed it to successfully avoid privacy incidents to date, are carried into the future.

---

[29]DHS defines "privacy incident" as "the loss of control, compromise, unauthorized disclosure, unauthorized acquisition, unauthorized access, or any similar term referring to situations where persons other than authorized users, have access or potential access to PII in usable form, whether physical or electronic, or where authorized users access PII for an unauthorized purpose. The term encompasses both suspected and confirmed incidents involving PII which raise a reasonable risk of harm."

[30]TSA Secure Flight and privacy officials also stated that there has not been any unauthorized access of PII, unauthorized PII collection, breaches of data-sharing agreements, or phishing or social engineering.

[31]GAO/AIMD-00-21.3.1.

DHS TRIP Addresses Inconveniences and Delays Related to TSDB-Based Lists, and Is Taking Actions to Reduce Case Processing Time

Passengers who, through the DHS TRIP redress process, are determined to have been misidentified to a TSDB-based high-risk list are added to the TSA Cleared List, which allows them to be cleared (not identified as high risk) nearly 100 percent of time.[32] The DHS TRIP process also allows passengers determined to have been either improperly placed or no longer appropriate for inclusion on a list (mislisted) to be removed from a TSDB-based list, reducing the likelihood they will be identified as matches during future travels.[33] DHS TRIP is not able to provide redress for passengers who may have been misidentified to high-risk, rules-based lists and subsequently applied to DHS TRIP for redress. However, according to TSA officials, TSA has taken steps to mitigate impacts on these passengers. DHS has also reduced its average processing time for redress cases, and is taking actions to reduce processing times for appeals cases.

---

[32]Because of the application of other TSA security measures, such as random selection, an individual's presence on the Cleared List may diminish, but will not preclude, the possibility of being selected for enhanced screening.

[33]During the pendency of this review, various courts have issued decisions relating to the No Fly List and DHS TRIP. For example, in January 2014, a judge of the U.S. District Court for the Northern District of California issued a findings of fact, conclusions of law, and order for relief in the case of *Ibrahim v. Dep't of Homeland Security*, No. C 06-00545 WHA (N.D. Cal. Jan 14, 2014) (redacted). Specifically, the court found that in this matter, which involved facts dating back to 2004, the plaintiff had been placed on the No Fly List as a result of an FBI agent's human error and that, among other things, the redress response letter provided to plaintiff by the redress program in place prior the establishment of DHS TRIP was inadequate at the time because the response was vague and "fell short of providing any assurance to [the Plaintiff]...that the mistake had been traced down in all its forms and venues and corrected." In June 2014, a judge of the U.S. District Court for the District of Oregon issued an opinion and order concluding, among other things, that because DHS TRIP procedures do not afford individuals the requirements of due process in so much as it does not provide them with notice regarding their status on the No Fly List and the reasons for placement on the list, "the absence of any meaningful procedures to afford Plaintiffs the opportunity to contest their placement on the No Fly List violates Plaintiffs' rights to procedural due process." See *Latif v. Holder*, No. 3:10-cv-00750-BR (D. Or. June 24, 2014). Our review focused on the procedures and data relating to implementation of the DHS TRIP redress and appeals processes and did not evaluate DHS TRIP on sufficiency of procedural due process grounds.

DHS TRIP Provides Passengers an Opportunity to Seek Redress for Impacts Associated with TSDB-Based Lists, and TSA Procedures for Using Rules-Based Lists Mitigate Impacts Associated with Being Misidentified

Passengers may be inconvenienced, delayed, or denied boarding because of Secure Flight vetting if they are misidentified to a watchlist record, meaning that Secure Flight matched their SFPD to a watchlist record that does not, upon further review, relate to the passenger; or mislisted, meaning that Secure Flight correctly identified the passenger as the subject of a watchlist record, but either the passenger should have a different watchlist status (e.g., should be included on the Selectee List rather than the No Fly List), or should not be included on a watchlist based upon the most current information.[34] The specific impacts experienced by a passenger who has been matched to a watchlist vary depending upon the list to which the passenger is matched. For example, an individual with a name similar to someone who is on the No Fly list likely will be unable to utilize the convenience of Internet, curbside, and airport kiosk check-in options.

Redress for TSDB-Based Lists

DHS TRIP affords passengers adversely affected by TSA screening processes an opportunity to address inconveniences and delays associated with being potentially misidentified to a TSDB-based list (the No Fly, Selectee, and Expanded Selectee Lists) and, if appropriate, to be added to the TSA Cleared List. If added to the TSA Cleared List, passengers who correctly use their redress control numbers when making a reservation should not experience delays and inconveniences associated with being misidentified to a TSDB-based list. As of February 2014, there were approximately 135,000 individuals included on the TSA Cleared List. According to Secure Flight performance data for fiscal years 2012 through 2013, passengers on the TSA Cleared List who correctly submitted their redress control numbers when making a travel reservation

---

[34]As of February 2014, Secure Flight officials were not aware of any passengers who have been misidentified to the CDC Do Not Board List. DHS TRIP officials stated that any inquiries related to the CDC Do Not Board List are forwarded to CDC for adjudication. Secure Flight officials were also unaware of any misidentifications to the TSA Pre✓™ Disqualification List. A person misidentified to the TSA Pre✓™ Disqualification List would be precluded from receiving the benefit of expedited screening, but would not be subjected to enhanced screening as a result of this misidentification. According to Secure Flight officials, Secure Flight is not developing a redress process for the TSA Pre✓™ Disqualification List because the matching algorithm for the list was designed in such a way as to ensure minimal risk of misidentification. According to TSA officials, TSA also has a process for responding to individuals who have questions about their TSA Pre✓™ status and individuals who TSA has disqualified from TSA Pre✓™ eligibility who want to request that TSA reconsider its decision.

were automatically cleared nearly 100 percent of the time by the Secure Flight system.[35]

DHS TRIP also affords passengers an opportunity to address inconveniences and delays associated with being potentially mislisted on a TSDB-based watchlist. As part of its review of DHS TRIP applicants who are found to be actual matches to the No Fly, Selectee, or Expanded Selectee Lists, TSC reviews whether the individuals currently meet criteria for inclusion on these lists. In some cases, TSC finds that the individual does not meet the criteria for inclusion, and the individual is removed from the list (delisted).[36] According to DHS TRIP data for fiscal years 2011 through 2013, the program received about 20,000 new, complete TSA-related redress applications and forwarded about 10 percent of these to TSC for review because the individuals seeking redress were a close or exact match to an individual on one of the TSDB-based lists.[37] During fiscal years 2011 through 2013, according to TSC data, screening agencies (including TSA) referred a total of 2,058 DHS TRIP applications to TSC for review.[38] Over the same time period, TSC confirmed that 1,333 DHS TRIP applicants matched the No Fly, Selectee, or Expanded Selectee lists, and delisted about 95 of these individuals. According to TSC officials, TSC will delist an individual when TSC analysts reviewing the case find the most current information available indicates the individual should be removed from the list. In addition, according to a DHS TRIP official, all delisted individuals are added to the

---

[35]To experience the benefit of being on the TSA Cleared List, passengers must submit their full name and date of birth, as provided to DHS TRIP, in addition to their redress control number when making a reservation.

[36]TSC conducts the review to determine whether the individual meets the criteria for inclusion on a TSDB-derived watchlist in accordance with TSC's standard operating procedures for redress.

[37]DHS TRIP forwards all redress applicants matching the No Fly, Selectee, or Expanded Selectee List to TSC, on behalf of TSA (the screening agency). Other federal entities with a redress function, such as the Department of State or U.S. Customs and Border Protection, conduct their own investigations of DHS TRIP applications involving their screening activities.

[38]TSC does not keep data on the number of DHS TRIP applications it reviews by agency; therefore, the 2,058 DHS TRIP applications TSC reviewed over fiscal years 2011 through 2013 could include applications forwarded to TSC from other screening agencies. Furthermore, according to TSC, because of the time frames associated with TSC's review process, the total number of TSA-related cases TSC reviewed during fiscal years 2011 through 2013 is less than the number of those forwarded to it by TSA.

TSA Cleared List, which reduces the likelihood they will be identified as matches to TSDB-based lists during future travels, thereby addressing any delays or inconveniences they may have experienced because of Secure Flight watchlist matching against such lists.

TSA Efforts to Mitigate Impacts Caused by Rules-Based Lists

DHS TRIP is not able to provide redress for passengers who may have been misidentified to high-risk, rules-based lists and subsequently applied to DHS TRIP for redress. However, according to TSA officials, TSA procedures for using the high-risk, rules-based lists mitigate impacts on passengers who may have been misidentified to these lists. These officials stated that there is a possibility that a passenger could be misidentified to a rules-based list if their name and date of birth are similar to those of an individual on the list. TSA has established procedures for using the rules-based lists to mitigate impacts on passengers from screening against the lists. These procedures could assist those misidentified as a result of Secure Flight screening and may result in TSA removing passengers from the lists.[39] By removing individuals from rules-based lists, TSA ensures that passengers who are misidentified to those individuals will no longer be identified as a match, and thus delayed or inconvenienced as a result. In certain circumstances, TSA also reviews questionable matches to the rules-based lists to determine whether individuals on the list should be removed. According to TSA officials, starting in 2012, TSA's Office of Intelligence and Analysis (OIA) began monitoring the number of questionable matches to the list. According to TSA officials, the rate of questionable matches is less than 1 percent of all matches to the list for April 2012 through May 2014. TSA officials stated that the TSA Intelligence Analysis Division manually reviews these questionable matches and removes individuals from the list who have been erroneously included on the list. By removing these individuals from the list, TSA ensures that passengers will no longer be erroneously matched to them, and thus delayed or inconvenienced as a result. However, according to TSA officials, TSA's effort to identify and remove questionable matches does not address all possible misidentifications to the rules-based list. For example, TSA officials stated they do not review some matches because TSA does not have additional information about those passengers—beyond that included in the SFPD—that would be necessary to determine whether the passenger was actually misidentified to the rules-based high-risk list.

---

[39]The details of these procedures are considered sensitive security information.

DHS Has Reduced Its Average Processing Time for Redress Cases, and Is Taking Actions to Reduce Processing Times for Appeals Cases

In fiscal year 2013, DHS TRIP officials began working to reduce overall processing time and the backlog of redress and appeals cases. As described previously, the DHS TRIP redress process involves adding applicants found not to be individuals on a TSDB-based list to the TSA Cleared List. At the conclusion of the redress process, certain individuals who apply to DHS TRIP receive a letter informing them there has been no change to their record and providing instructions on how to appeal the decision.[40] This additional process—known as the appeals process—involves an additional set of activities carried out by the appellant (the redress applicant submitting the appeal), DHS TRIP, and TSC. The process begins when the appellant files the appeal, and DHS TRIP forwards all completed appeals paperwork to TSC, as shown in figure 1. Once TSC receives the documentation, TSC analysts are to review all derogatory information maintained on the appellant to make a written recommendation to TSA on the appeal.[41] TSA then reviews TSC's recommendation through its own internal process, which can include going back to TSC for additional information, before the TSA Administrator makes the final determination to uphold the appellant's status, recommend that TSC downgrade the appellant to another TSDB-based list, or recommend that TSC remove the appellant from the list.[42]

---

[40]These individuals then have 30 days from the receipt of the decision to submit an appeal, after which, failure to file an appeal will result in the decision becoming a final agency decision.

[41]According to TSC officials, analysts within TSC's Redress Unit conduct the initial review for a redress application; analysts within TSC's Office of Intelligence and Analysis conduct reviews for all appeals. According to TSC officials, analysts in both offices follow the same procedures to conduct these reviews.

[42]TSC, in the course of its review, may also find the appellant was misidentified to a TSDB-based list.

Figure 1: Department of Homeland Security (DHS) Traveler Redress Inquiry Program (TRIP) Redress and Appeals Process

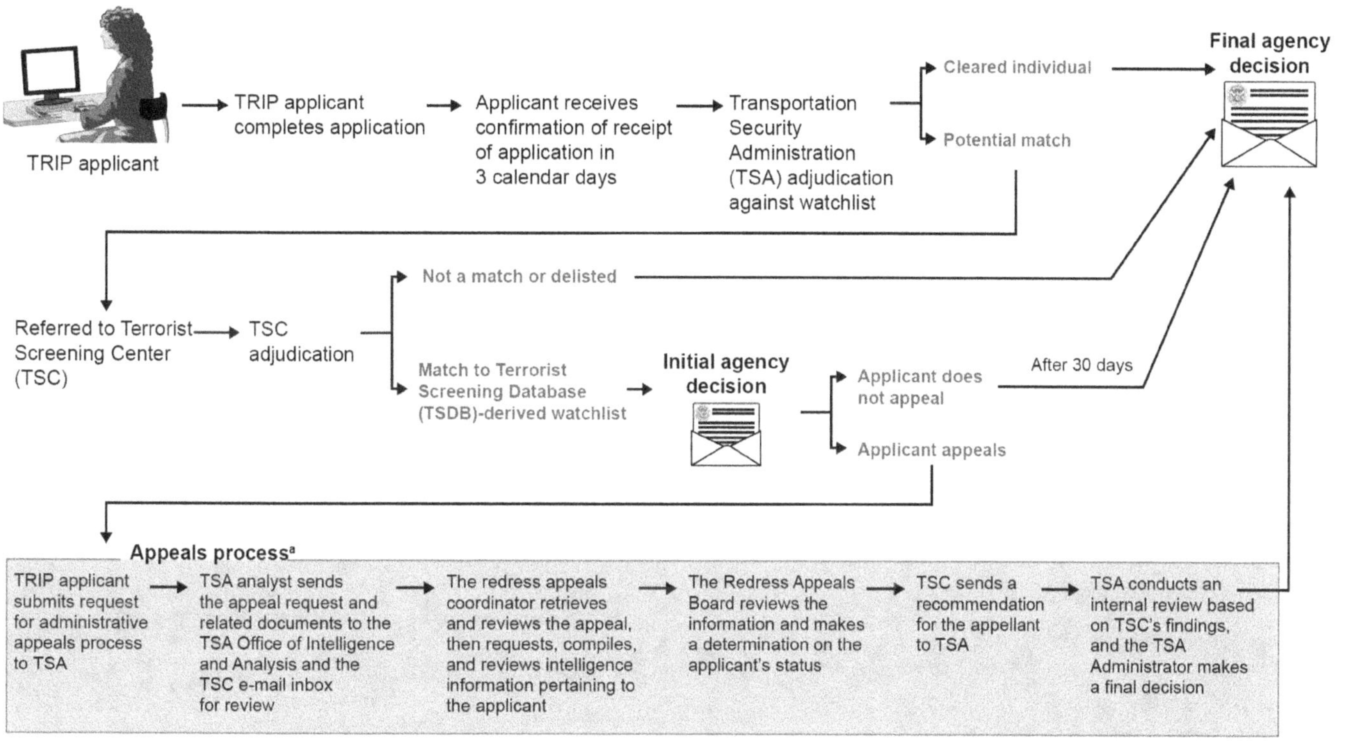

Source: GAO; TSA (logo); Art Explosion (clip art). | GAO-14-647

^aSome passengers are not permitted to appeal the agency decision. The specific types of passengers who are permitted to appeal are considered law enforcement sensitive/sensitive security information.

Redress Process

With respect to the redress process, DHS TRIP officials took several steps in fiscal year 2013 to reduce the overall processing time and a backlog of redress cases. First, in fiscal year 2013, DHS automated its response to DHS TRIP applicants, a step that, according to DHS TRIP, should reduce the initial response time from 3 days to 1 day. Second, DHS hired additional staff for DHS TRIP, achieving its authorized staffing level of 11 full-time positions. Third, in January 2013, DHS TRIP implemented and began training staff on a new redress case management system, the Redress Management System (RMS). As part of the migration of the data from the prior system to RMS, DHS TRIP administratively closed approximately 30,000 cases that were either duplicates or incomplete because documentation was never received from the applicant. The new system also includes reporting capabilities that enable DHS TRIP to generate reports used to monitor its performance in meeting its performance targets. Fourth, DHS TRIP created and filled a DHS TRIP Operations Manager position with the intent that this individual would increase the office's focus on developing, analyzing, and monitoring performance metrics.[43] According to DHS TRIP officials, at the beginning of fiscal year 2014, DHS TRIP's average case-processing time for redress cases was about 100 days, and as of June 2014, the average case-processing time was about 42 days.

Consistent with its efforts to reduce processing time for redress, in January 2014, DHS TRIP reduced its target for one of the department's key performance indicators—average number of days for DHS TRIP redress cases to be closed—from 93 to 78 days.[44]

Appeals Process

DHS also took action in fiscal year 2013 to address timeframes associated with the appeals process. Appeals applicants receive a letter stating that DHS will provide a final agency decision on the appeal within 60 days of receipt of the appeal. However, the average total processing time for the appeals process for fiscal years 2011 through 2013 was 276 days, as shown in table 2.

---

[43]DHS TRIP is also planning to implement two customer feedback surveys. The first survey, which will be administered at the time an individual is applying for redress, will solicit applicants' views on their experience during the DHS TRIP process. The second survey, which will be administered 90 days after the final agency decision letter is provided, will gather information on passenger experiences using the redress control number. As of July 2014, both surveys were under review by OMB. According to DHS officials, the program plans to begin administering the survey as soon as OMB completes its review.

[44]This performance target is used to measure DHS's progress in meeting one of the department's three priority goals—to strengthen aviation security counterterrorism capabilities by using intelligence-driven information and risk-based decisions. DHS TRIP revised the performance target for TSA-only redress cases, that is, cases that do not involve any other DHS components, from an average total processing time of 43 days to 20 days.

Table 2: Average Processing Time Frames for Key Phases of Closed Appeals Cases Received during Fiscal Years 2011-2013 (n=49)[a]

Processing data point	Mean (in days)	Range (in days)
Time between receipt of complete appeal by DHS TRIP and the submission of appeal by DHS TRIP to TSC	33	1-603
Time between TSC's receipt of complete appeal and its recommendation to TSA	154[b]	8-811
Time between TSC's recommendation to TSA and the closing of the appeal	89	1-832
Total processing time (Covers time period from the date DHS TRIP received the complete appeal to the date the appeal was closed)	276	28-1023

Source: GAO analysis of DHS TR P appeals case data. | GAO-14-647SU

[a]According to DHS TRIP data, as of July 16, 2014, 5 additional appeals cases received during fiscal years 2011 and 2013 remained open.

[b]According to TSC data for these 49 cases, the average number of days to complete TSC's review (i.e., the time between TSC's receipt of the complete appeal and its recommendation to TSA) was 130 days, as opposed to the 154 days based on DHS TRIP data. TSC and DHS TRIP officials attributed this difference to inconsistent record keeping between the two agencies for recording the sent and received dates for the cases. DHS TRIP officials also noted that data transmission errors delayed TSC's receipt of some cases. As discussed later in this report, the agencies are taking steps to improve communication regarding appeals cases.

In fiscal year 2013, DHS TRIP began taking several actions to make the appeals process more structured and reduce the overall review time. To provide a more structured appeals process, DHS TRIP took the following steps:

- It created an appeals team to manage both the intelligence analysis and the administrative aspects of appeals.
- It developed and began distributing a document that provides information on the status and, if available, outcome of each appeal case.
- It implemented a more formalized process for reviewing appeals. This process includes distributing appeal information to TSC, TSA OIA, and TSA's Office of Chief Counsel and conducting pre-meetings among stakeholders, including TSA OIA, TSA's Office of Chief Counsel, and DHS TRIP; meetings with TSA leadership; and, as appropriate, a decision meeting with the TSA Administrator.
- It developed a draft of the Functional Roles and Responsibilities Document (formerly known as the DHS TRIP standard operating

procedures), which outlines the role of DHS TRIP officials in the appeals process.[45]

- It developed and implemented a database to track appeals specifically and improve process timeliness.

Additionally, in January 2014, DHS TRIP officials stated they were reviewing TSC's appeals standard operating procedures to identify opportunities for the agencies to further reduce time frames. According to DHS TRIP officials, as of May 2014, the program director had completed a review of TSC's appeals standard operating procedures, provided metrics on TSC's timeliness, and provided suggestions to TSC for reducing its time frames. TSC officials also stated that they meet monthly with DHS TRIP to discuss opportunities to improve efficiency and reduce time frames. From fiscal year 2011—the first fiscal year in which DHS TRIP received a redress appeal—through fiscal year 2013, for appeals closed within that period, the average number of days, according to DHS TRIP data, for TSC to review an appeal package and submit a recommendation to TSA was about 154 days, as shown in table 2. Therefore, TSC's review accounted for over half (154 of 276 days) of the total review time. In addition, DHS TRIP is working to further reduce processing times for other parts of the appeals process. Specifically, according to DHS TRIP officials, DHS TRIP has committed to reducing the number of meetings with TSA's Office of Chief Counsel and TSA OIA. In addition, for those meetings that do take place, DHS TRIP officials and TSA leadership are anticipating questions from participants that could delay the appeal's progress through the system because they require significant follow-up, and working to obtain the answers in advance.

In addition, in January 2014, DHS TRIP established intermediate and long-term performance goals for the appeals process for the first time. Specifically, the intermediate performance goal calls for an average total processing time of 92 days, while the long-term performance goal calls for an average processing time of 60 days, consistent with the time frame DHS TRIP commits to achieving in the letter informing applicants of their right to appeal. According to DHS TRIP officials, the agency plans to periodically assess its progress toward achieving its intermediate and long-term goals for reducing appeals-processing times. Officials stated that if DHS TRIP finds it is not making adequate progress by February 2015—about 1 year after the program began taking specific actions to

---

[45]The Functional Roles and Responsibilities Document was finalized in January 2014.

reduce the overall review time—it would first evaluate whether further changes and improvements could be made to shorten the appeals process before considering, in collaboration with TSC and the DHS Screening Coordination Office, a change to the 60-day time frame stated in the appeals letter.

Conclusions

The Secure Flight program is one of TSA's key tools for defending commercial flights against terrorist threats. However, because the program relies on sensitive information, including personally identifiable information from the approximately 2 million people Secure Flight screens each day, privacy incidents and inappropriate disclosures could have significant negative impacts on the traveling public. Since TSA began implementing Secure Flight, in 2009, the program has made significant progress in addressing privacy protections. TSA could further strengthen these protections by providing job-specific privacy refresher training consistent with OMB requirements. Furthermore, developing a mechanism to comprehensively document and track key Secure Flight privacy-related issues and decisions could help TSA ensure that its oversight of privacy protections is effective and that the decisions that have allowed it to successfully avoid privacy incidents to date are carried into the future. DHS TRIP and TSC have also made progress in addressing Secure Flight misidentifications to TSDB-based lists, and their planned actions for reducing redress and appeals case-processing time could further improve the redress process. It will be important for DHS TRIP to conduct its assessments of performance data as planned to determine whether further changes to the appeals process, such as changes to the time frames presented in DHS's appeals letter, are warranted.

Recommendations for Executive Action

We recommend that the Transportation Security Administration's Administrator take the following two actions:

- to further protect personally identifiable information in the Secure Flight system, provide job-specific privacy refresher training for Secure Flight staff, and
- to ensure Secure Flight has complete information for effective oversight of its privacy controls, develop a mechanism to comprehensively document and track key Secure Flight privacy issues and decisions.

Agency Comments

We provided a draft of this report to DHS and the Department of Justice for their review and comment. DHS provided written comments on July 17, 2014, which are summarized below and reproduced in full in appendix II. DHS concurred with both of our two recommendations and described planned actions to address them. In addition, DHS provided written technical comments, which we incorporated into the report as appropriate.

DHS concurred with our first recommendation that TSA provide job-specific privacy refresher training for Secure Flight staff. DHS stated that TSA's OIA will develop and deliver job-specific privacy refresher training for all Secure Flight staff. TSA plans to complete this effort by December 31, 2014. These actions, if implemented effectively, should address our recommendation and help further protect personally identifiable information in the Secure Flight system.

DHS also concurred with our second recommendation that TSA develop a mechanism to comprehensively document and track key Secure Flight privacy issues and decisions. DHS noted that TSA's OIA currently identifies and addresses privacy issues through the efforts of privacy personnel within TSA and those embedded within the Secure Flight program and stated that TSA will develop a mechanism for documenting and tracking key Secure Flight privacy issues and decisions. TSA plans to complete this effort by March 31, 2015. This action, if implemented effectively, will help ensure Secure Flight has complete information for effective oversight of its privacy controls. We will continue to monitor DHS's efforts.

The Department of Justice did not have formal comments on our draft report, but provided technical comments, which we incorporated as appropriate.

As agreed with your office, unless you publicly announce the contents of this report earlier, we plan no further distribution until 30 days from the report date. At that time, we will send copies of this report to the Secretary of Homeland Security, the TSA Administrator, the Attorney General, and appropriate congressional committees. The report is also available at no charge on the GAO website at http://www.gao.gov.

Should you or your staff have any questions about this report, please contact Jennifer A. Grover at 202-512-7141 or GroverJ@gao.gov. Key contributors to this report are acknowledged in appendix III. Key points for our Office of Congressional Relations and Public Affairs may be found on the last page of this report.

Jennifer A. Grover
Director
Homeland Security and Justice Issues

Appendix I: Fair Information Practices Principles

Since December 2008, it has been Department of Homeland Security (DHS) policy to follow the Fair Information Practices Principles (FIPPs). The FIPPs, a set of principles first proposed in 1973 by a U.S. government advisory committee, are used with some variation by organizations to address privacy considerations in their business practices and are also the basis of privacy laws and related policies in many countries, including the United States, Australia, and New Zealand, and in the European Union. DHS's privacy policy guidance lists eight FIPPs:[1]

- **Transparency:** DHS should be transparent and provide notice to the individual regarding its collection, use, dissemination, and maintenance of personally identifiable information (PII).[2]
- **Individual participation:** DHS should involve the individual in the process of using PII and, to the extent practicable, seek individual consent for the collection, use, dissemination, and maintenance of PII. DHS should also provide mechanisms for appropriate access, correction, and redress regarding DHS's use of PII.
- **Purpose specification:** DHS should specifically articulate the authority that permits the collection of PII and specifically articulate the purpose or purposes for which the PII is intended to be used.
- **Data minimization:** DHS should collect only PII that is directly relevant and necessary to accomplish the specified purpose(s) and retain PII only as long as is necessary to fulfill the specified purpose(s).
- **Use limitation:** DHS should use PII solely for the purpose(s) specified in the notice. Sharing PII outside the department should be for a purpose compatible with the purpose for which the PII was collected.
- **Data quality and integrity:** DHS should, to the extent practicable, ensure that PII is accurate, relevant, timely, and complete.
- **Security:** DHS should protect PII (in all media) through appropriate security safeguards against risks such as loss, unauthorized access

---

[1]DHS, *The Fair Information Practice Principles: Framework for Privacy Policy at the Department of Homeland Security,* DHS Privacy Policy Guidance Memorandum 2008-01 (Washington, D.C., Dec. 29, 2008).

[2]PII is any information that permits the identity of an individual to be directly or indirectly inferred, including other information that is linked or linkable to an individual. See DHS, *Privacy Policy and Compliance,* DHS Instruction 047-01-001 (Washington, D.C.: July 25, 2011).

GAO-14-647 TSA Secure Flight Privacy

or use, destruction, modification, or unintended or inappropriate
disclosure.

- **Accountability and auditing:** DHS should be accountable for
complying with these principles, providing training to all employees
and contractors who use PII, and auditing the actual use of PII to
demonstrate compliance with these principles and all applicable
privacy protection requirements.

Appendix II: Comments from the Department of Homeland Security

U.S. Department of Homeland Security
Washington, DC 20528

July 17, 2014

Jennifer A. Grover
Director, Homeland Security and Justice Issues
U.S. Government Accountability Office
441 G Street, NW
Washington, DC 20548

Re: Draft Report GAO-14-647, "SECURE FLIGHT: TSA Could Take Additional Steps to Strengthen Privacy Oversight Mechanisms"

Dear Ms. Grover:

Thank you for the opportunity to review and comment on the draft report referenced above. The U.S. Department of Homeland Security (DHS) appreciates the U.S. Government Accountability Office's (GAO's) work in planning and conducting its review and issuing this report.

The Department is pleased to note GAO's recognition that the Transportation Security Administration (TSA) has "made significant progress in addressing privacy protections" since it began implementing the Secure Flight program in 2009. TSA has strengthened Secure Flight by moving from a program that identified high risk passengers by matching them against Government watch lists, to one that uses the information that TSA has historically collected to assign all passengers a risk category: high risk, low risk, or unknown risk. TSA has also enhanced Secure Flight's privacy oversight mechanisms to protect personally identifiable information. Secure Flight continues to be the Nation's frontline defense against terrorism that may target the Nation's civil aviation system. It is a very effective tool in identifying individuals who should be kept off aircraft, subjected to enhanced screening prior to boarding an aircraft, or who should be given expedited screening.

The draft report contained two recommendations with which the Department concurs. Specifically, GAO recommended that the TSA Administrator:

Recommendation 1: Provide job-specific privacy refresher training for Secure Flight staff.

Response: Concur. TSA's Office of Intelligence and Analysis (OIA) currently provides specialized privacy training to Secure Flight personnel during employee on-boarding but will develop and deliver job-specific privacy refresher training for all Secure Flight staff. Estimated Completion Date (ECD): December 31, 2014.

Recommendation 2: Develop a mechanism to comprehensively document and track key Secure Flight privacy issues and decisions.

Response: Concur. TSA's OIA currently identifies and addresses privacy issues through the comprehensive efforts of privacy personnel within TSA and those embedded within the Secure Flight program. These personnel are placed in positions that provide for complete insight into program direction and developments. TSA will develop a mechanism for documenting and tracking key Secure Flight privacy issues and decisions. ECD: March 31, 2015.

Again, thank you for the opportunity to review and comment on this draft report. Technical comments were previously provided under separate cover. Please feel free to contct me if you have any questions. We look forward to working with you in the future.

Sincerely,

Jim H. Crumpacker, CIA, CFE
Director
Departmental GAO-OIG Liaison Office

2

Appendix III: GAO Contact and Staff Acknowledgments

GAO Contact	Jennifer A. Grover, 202-512-7141, GroverJ@gao.gov
Staff Acknowledgments	In addition to the contact named above, Maria Strudwick (Assistant Director), Ashley Vaughan (Analyst-in-Charge), Mona Nichols Blake, John de Ferrari, Michele Fejfar, Imoni Hampton, Eric Hauswirth, Susan Hsu, Richard Hung, Justine Lazaro, Tom Lombardi, Linda Miller, and David Plocher made key contributions to this report.